beadwork

beadwork

Home decorating with beads

Lisa Brown

Photography by Lucinda Symons

southwater

This edition published by Southwater

Distributed in the USA by
Ottenheimer Publishing
5 Park Center Court
Suite 300
Owing Mills MD 2117-5001, USA
tel. (001) 410 902 9100
fax. (001) 410 902 7210

Distributed in the UK by
The Manning Partnership
251-253 London Road East
Batheaston, Bath BA1 7RL, UK
tel. (0044) 01225 852 727
fax. (0044) 01225 852 852

Distributed in Australia by
Sandstone Publishing
Unit 1, 360 Norton Street, Leichhardt,
New South Wales, Australia
tel. (0061) 2 9560 7888
fax. (0061) 2 9560 7488

Distributed in New Zealand by
Five Mile Press NZ
Unit 3/46a Taharoto Road, PO Box 33-1071
Takapuna, Auckland 9, New Zealand
tel. (0064) 9 486 1925
fax. (0064) 9 486 1454

Southwater is an imprint of
Anness Publishing Limited
© 1998, 2000 Anness Publishing Limited

1 3 5 7 9 10 8 6 4 2
Printed and bound in China
Previously published as Inspirations: Decorating with Beads

Publisher: Joanna Lorenz
Senior Editor: Lindsay Porter
Designer: Ian Sandon
Step Photographer: Rodney Forte
Stylist: Lisa Brown
Illustrators: Madeleine David and Lucinda Ganderton

CONTENTS

INTRODUCTION

Nothing adds a touch of glamour to ordinary textiles quite like beads - in the same way as a plain outfit can be transformed with a string of glittering beads, you can perk up your interiors with splashes of sparkle and colour. Today, beads are available in a wider range than ever before, from chunky wooden beads stained in earthy tones to lustrous Venetian glass.

This book provides over 20 practical projects showing you how to embellish every area of the home with beads large and small - from beautiful fringed edgings for cushions, to delicate bead curtains; sparkling picture frames to glitzy light fittings. If you collect beads, this book will inspire you to make the most of your treasures; if beads are new to you, it will open up a whole new realm of decorative possibilities.

Techniques range from appliqué and using a bead loom to couching, threading, and even gluing in place. All the methods used are included in the individual projects,

while an additional techniques section will allow you to perfect the more exacting skills required. For those who are unable to find just the right bead for the job, there are even suggestions for making your own. Whether stitched onto fabrics, suspended from light fittings or incorporated into a bathroom splashback, there is no more luxurious way to add sparkle to your home than with beads.

Deborah Barker

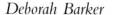

GIANT BEAD CORD-PULLS

If you possess some interesting large beads, cord-pulls are an ideal way to make the most of them: just one or two striking examples can be given real impact used this way, and you can have the satisfaction of using them every day.

YOU WILL NEED
extra-long pins
small silver rocaille beads
5 coloured resin beads
2 metal cones
wire cutters
round-nosed jewellery pliers
medium and fine silver wire
2 small round metal beads
extra-large metal bead
coloured leather thongs
ready-made tassel
2 hand-made foil-and-glass beads
tape measure
silk cord
stranded embroidery thread (floss)
2 large, dyed bone beads
strong non-stretch bead thread
4 long, bleached bone beads
8 small bone beads
satin ribbon
large, flat hand-made glass bead with large hole
needle and tacking (basting) thread

1 For the metal cord–pull, take an extra-long pin and thread with small silver rocaille beads and a large resin bead between two metal cones. Snip off the excess wire and bend the end into a small loop at the top. Take a length of medium silver wire, bend the end into a small loop and attach it to the top loop of the pendant.

2 Thread on two small silver rocailles, a small round metal bead, a resin bead, an extra-large metal bead, another resin bead, another small metal bead and two more silver rocailles. Snip off the excess wire and bend into a loop at the top.

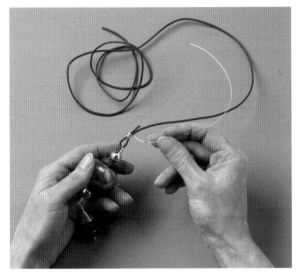

3 Thread a coloured leather thong through the loop, fold the thong back on itself and bind securely together with fine silver wire.

4 To make the tassel cord-pull, bend one end of a length of medium silver wire around the small cord loop at the top of a tassel. Pass the wire through two foil-and-glass beads, snip off the wire about 1.5 cm/⅝ in above the top bead and use pliers to bend it into a small loop.

5 Pass the end of a length of matching silk cord through the loop, fold it back on itself and bind securely with embroidery thread (floss).

6 For the decorative bone cord-pull, thread a large bone bead onto an extra-long pin between two coloured resin beads. Use pliers to bend the end of the pin into a small loop.

7 Take a short piece of medium silver wire, bend a small loop in one end and pass through a second large bone bead. Snip off the wire and bend it into a loop at the top. ▶

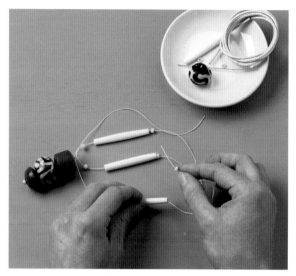

8 Tie two strands of strong non-stretch bead thread to the wire loop at the top of the group of beads, leaving four long ends. Thread each through a small bone bead followed by a long bleached bone bead and finally another small bone bead.

9 Tie the threads securely to the wire loop under the top bead and thread the ends back through the bone beads to conceal them. Pass a leather thong through the topmost wire loop, fold it back on itself and bind with wire as in step 3.

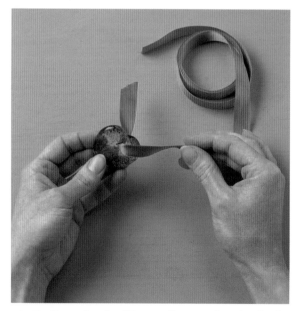

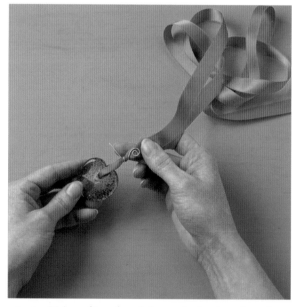

10 For a simple ribbon-pull, pass a length of satin ribbon through the hole in a large, flat hand-made glass bead. Double the ribbon back on itself and tack (baste) in place close to the top of the bead.

11 Using pliers, bend the end of a short length of medium silver wire into a small spiral, then use the rest to bind around the ribbon.

SIMPLE BEAD CURTAIN

A bead curtain hung across the kitchen door is a tried and tested way to deter insects on a hot, sunny day. This jaunty striped version is quick and cheap to make, combining wooden and plastic beads with coloured drinking straws.

YOU WILL NEED
wire cutters
2–3 large spools of plastic-coated jewellery wire
tape measure
large, flat glass beads with central hole
large and medium plastic beads
large, medium and small wooden beads
scissors
coloured and striped plastic drinking straws
pencil
length of 2.5 cm/1 in wooden batten to fit inside door frame
drill
staple gun

1 Cut a length of wire to fit the door length plus 25 cm/10 in, and tie one end to a large glass bead, which will act as a weight at the bottom.

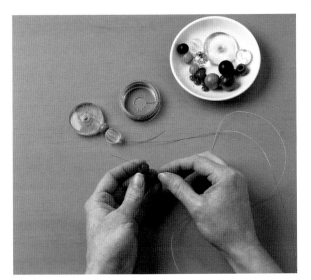

2 Thread on a large plastic bead between two medium wooden beads to cover the knot.

3 Using scissors, cut the drinking straws into 7.5 cm/3 in lengths.

4 Thread on three lengths of straw, alternating plain with striped, and threading a small wooden bead in between each.

5 Thread on a group of medium and large beads and repeat the sequence, using assorted colours, to fill the wire. Make more strands to complete the curtain.

6 Mark and drill holes at 2.5 cm/1 in intervals all along the batten, plus a screw hole at each end.

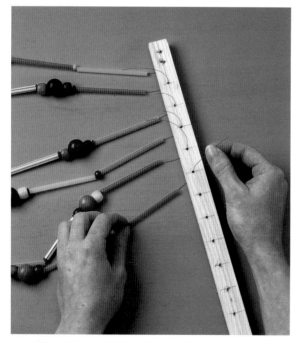

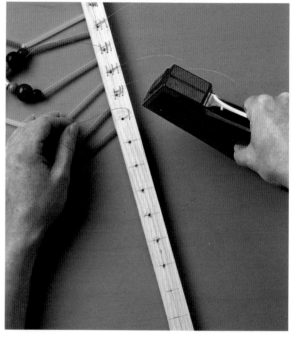

7 Thread the end of each wire through one of the holes in the batten.

8 Use a staple gun to secure the beaded threads to the batten.

BEADED WIRE CANDLESTICKS

Twisted silver wire, sparingly threaded with beads, has a delicate yet sculptural quality. An assortment of decorative glass beads, following a colour theme, attracts the light and looks wonderful entwining a pair of glass candlesticks.

YOU WILL NEED
tape meaure
wire cutters
medium silver wire
pair of glass candlesticks
round-nosed jewellery pliers
medium decorative glass beads in yellow, green,
silver and clear
pen or pencil
small glass rocaille beads and square beads in
complementary shades

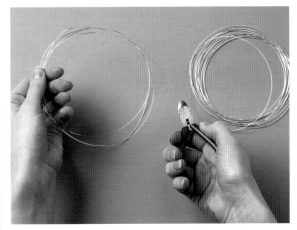

1 Cut four 1 m/40 in lengths of medium silver wire for each candlestick.

2 Bend a loop at the end of the first length and thread on a decorative bead.

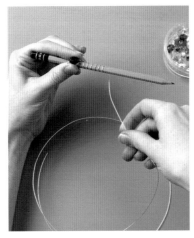

3 Wind the end of the wire around a pen or pencil six times to form a spiral.

4 Thread on about eight small glass beads and divide them among the loops. Thread on another medium-sized bead and repeat, forming spirals and threading beads until you reach the end ▶ of the wire.

5 When you reach the end of the wire, use the pliers to twist the end.

6 Thread on the final decorative bead and finish with a loop at the end of the wire.

7 Make up the other three spirals in the same way, distributing the coloured beads evenly among the loops.

8 Wrap two spiral lengths around the stem of each candlestick to form an interesting shape. Secure the spirals in place by binding them gently to the stem with more wire.

FINE BEAD CURTAIN

A bead curtain will allow you to guard your privacy while letting in all available light. This one is made up of lengths of transparent nylon line threaded with glass and silver beads that will glitter prettily in the sunlight at your window.

YOU WILL NEED
pencil
ruler
length of 2.5 cm/1 in wooden batten to fit
across window
tape measure
nylon fishing line
scissors
large, flat glass beads with central hole, in two colours
strong glue
silver bugle beads
silver rocaille beads
silver square beads
assorted large glass beads
staple gun
2.5 cm/1 in wide ribbon
beading needle and matching thread

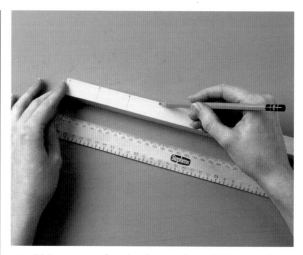

1 Using a pencil and ruler, mark equidistant points about 4 cm/1½ in apart along the length of the wooden batten.

2 Measure the window from top to bottom and cut lengths of nylon fishing line to this measurement plus 20 cm/8 in to allow for knotting. You will need one length of fishing line for each mark on the batten.

3 Prepare the strands of the curtain one at a time. Thread on a large, flat glass bead and tie a knot. Trim the excess line and then apply a blob of glue to the knot for extra security.

4 Thread on a selection of beads to a length of about 5 cm/2 in. Combine the silver bugles, silver rocailles and silver square beads with a large glass bead. From the top of this group, measure between 4 cm/1½ in and 8 cm/3¼ in along the line and make a knot. (Vary this length as you go, making some sections longer and some shorter.) Thread on another selection of beads to measure between 4 cm/1½ in and 8 cm/3¼ in in length. This time, thread the large bead in the centre of the smaller beads, which should be threaded symmetrically on either side of it. Continue as before until you reach the end of the length of nylon.

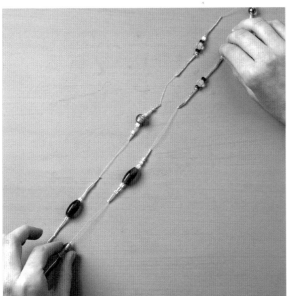

5 The next length will be slightly shorter than the first to create a staggered line at the bottom of the curtain. Lay the second length of nylon alongside the completed first length and, when threading this length, position the beads so that they roughly correspond with the beadless gaps on the first length.

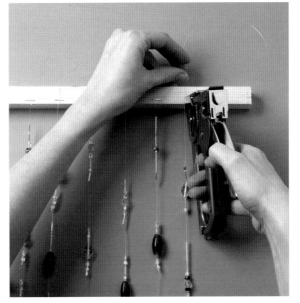

6 As you complete each length, tie a double knot at the top. Staple the lengths at the marked positions on the batten; the knot will act as an anchor above the staple. It's easier to do this in a hanging position to make sure the bottom of the curtain is level.

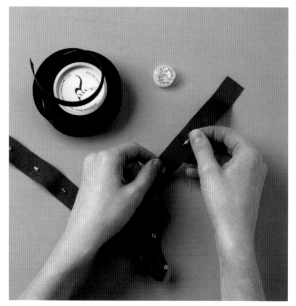

7 To hide the staples, the front of the batten needs covering. Cut a length of ribbon to the length of the batten plus 2 cm/¾ in. Decorate the ribbon by stitching a single row of beads along the middle.

8 Staple the ribbon in position at either end of the batten, hiding the staples.

NAPKIN RING AND NIGHT-LIGHT

Wired rocaille beads, woven into simple striped designs, shimmer in the candlelight and make delicate yet sumptuous ornaments for the dinner table. It is essential to use a night-light with its own metal container in the night-light holder.

YOU WILL NEED
fine galvanized wire
ruler or tape measure
wire cutters
round-nosed jewellery pliers
plastic bottle and beaker, to use as formers
glass rocaille beads in pink, red and orange
fine silver wire
adhesive pads

1 For the napkin ring, take about 2 m/2 yd of galvanized wire and bend a small loop in one end using pliers. Wind the wire about ten times around the plastic bottle or beaker.

2 Thread enough pink glass rocaille beads onto the wire to fit around the bottle or beaker once, then change to red and thread another round of beads.

3 Go on threading beads in this sequence until the wire is full, then use the pliers to bend another small loop in the end to prevent the beads falling off.

4 Bend the beaded wire around the bottle or beaker again to restore its shape. Secure a length of fine silver wire to the first row, then bind it around the others, keeping the spiral in shape. Do this at two or three other points around the napkin ring.

5 When the ring is complete, wind the ends of the silver wires back around the previous rows to neaten, and snip off the excess.

▶

6 To make the night-light holder, bend one end of a long piece of galvanized wire into a small loop as before. Thread the first part of the wire with orange glass rocailles.

7 Bend the beaded wire into a small spiral to form the base of the night-light holder. Attach two lengths of silver wire to the centre of the spiral and bind each row to the previous one to secure the shape. Thread on more beads if necessary until the base fits that of the plastic bottle or beaker.

8 Use adhesive pads to attach the beaded spiral base temporarily to the base of the bottle or beaker.

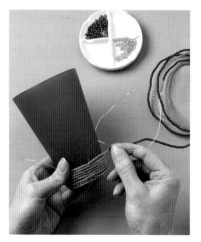

9 Join on more galvanized wire if necessary, by twisting the ends together with pliers. Then thread on enough orange rocailles to wind around the bottle or beaker about four or five times.

10 Wind the beaded wire around the bottle or beaker, binding each row to the last using the silver wire. Pull the wire quite tight to hold the shape.

11 Change to the red beads and repeat until the holder reaches the height you want. To finish, bind the silver wire a few times tightly around the beaded wire and back around the previous rows. Snip off the ends.

BEAD-ENCRUSTED FRAMES

There's nothing difficult about the method used to decorate these sparkly picture frames: treat small beads like glitter and simply pour them generously onto a glued surface. Use bold, clear colours underneath to enhance the beads.

YOU WILL NEED
medium-grade sandpaper
flat wooden picture frames
emulsion (latex) or acrylic paint
medium paintbrushes
saucer or palette
PVA (white) glue
small glass rocaille beads in a variety of colours
large sheet of paper
glitter
bugle beads in a variety of colours

1 Use medium-grade sandpaper to remove any old paint or varnish from the frames.

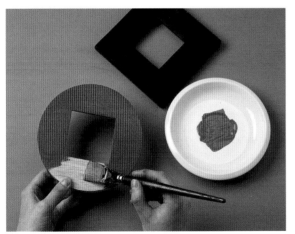

2 Paint each frame in a flat colour and allow to dry. Add another coat if necessary for even coverage.

3 Paint a heart shape in each corner of a square frame, using PVA (white) glue. Sprinkle rocaille beads generously over the glue, using a different colour for each heart, and press them down lightly. After the beads have settled for a minute or two, lightly tap the frame to remove any loose ones. ▶

4 Paint the rest of the frame with PVA glue. With the frame on a large sheet of paper, sprinkle on the glitter. Tap off the excess glitter and return it to the container.

5 Decorate a round frame using bugle beads in various shades of the same colour. Apply PVA glue around the centre of the frame and sprinkle on the beads.

6 Gradually work out to the edge of the frame, applying darker or lighter beads to produce a shaded effect.

7 Decorate a small frame by simply gluing assorted beads around the edges.

SILKEN KEY TASSELS

Hang these pretty tassels from keys in the bedroom or bathroom. Worked in colours that co-ordinate with the rest of the room's decor, they make charming decorative details.

YOU WILL NEED
2 skeins of stranded embroidery thread (floss) for each tassel,
plus extra for loops and ties
stiff card (cardboard)
scissors
tape measure
needle and matching thread
2 large ceramic beads
beading needle
small glass rocaille beads in red, orange and turquoise
large glass rocaille beads in red and turquoise
medium red glass crystals
small red opaque rocaille beads

1 Wind two skeins of stranded embroidery thread (floss) around a piece of card (cardboard).

2 Cut a 20 cm/8 in length of embroidery thread and tie it into a hanging loop, then tie the ends tightly around the top loop of the wound thread.

3 Remove the tied bundle from the card and cut through the lower loop to form the tassel.

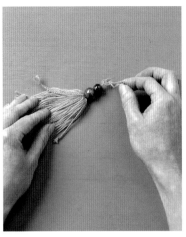

4 Separate six threads into three pairs and make a tight plait (braid). Use a needle and matching thread to secure the end. Make another three plaits in the same way around the tassel.

5 Trim the ends of the tassel evenly, to make a level fringe.

6 Thread the hanging loop at the top of the tassel through the two ceramic beads, then tie the loop in a small knot to secure.

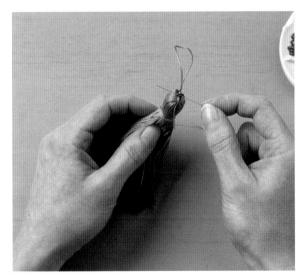

7 To make a beaded tassel, repeat steps 1–3, then tie a short length of thread around the bundle about 2 cm/¾ in down from the top to form a "waist". Stitch a length of thread to the top of the tassel and thread on eight small red rocailles. Tie off with a double knot to make a ring around the hanging loop.

8 Passing the thread through alternate rocailles in the previous round, make three loops, each consisting of two orange rocailles, two turquoise, two red and one large red rocaille, with the sequence reversed to complete the loop.

▶

9 Make another three loops following the same sequence as before but passing the thread through the large red rocailles of the previous round.

10 Link the large red rocailles added in step 9 with a row of six red rocailles between each, then repeat with a row of six orange rocailles.

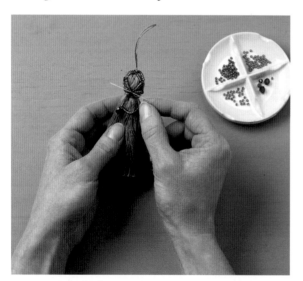

11 Link the large red rocailles again with six turquoise rocailles, then suspend a pendant loop from each large red bead. To make the pendant loop, thread three red, three turquoise, three orange rocailles and one red rocaille, then one medium red glass crystal and one small red opaque. Then pass the thread back through the last two beads and reverse the sequence for the other side of the loop.

12 Again passing the thread through the large red rocailles to link them, make three loops, each consisting of three red, three turquoise and three orange rocailles, one red rocaille, then one large turquoise rocaille and one small red opaque. For each, pass the thread back through the last two beads and reverse the sequence for the other side. Finish off the thread by tying a secure knot.

BEAD-TRIMMED VOILE JUG COVERS

This is a traditional idea that has never been bettered, and has now made a welcome come-back in the kitchen. Once you've made a few of these pretty and functional covers, you'll wonder what you did without them.

YOU WILL NEED
scissors
tape measure
checked and plain orange voile
needle and tacking (basting) thread
sewing machine
matching sewing thread
iron (optional)
dressmaker's pins
large orange plastic beads
medium pink frosted glass beads
small frosted glass beads in red and pink
small orange opaque glass rocaille beads
small square orange frosted glass beads
large orange frosted glass beads

1 Cut out a 20 cm/8 in diameter circle of fabric and tack (baste) a narrow double hem around the edge. Machine-stitch the hem close to the edge.

2 Fold the hemmed circle into quarters, then eighths, then sixteenths, and press the folds between your fingers or with an iron to divide the circle into equal sections.

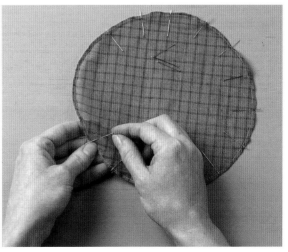

3 Mark each section of the fabric with a pin at the hemmed edge.

▶

33

4 Secure a length of matching thread to the hem at a pin marker, then thread on one large orange plastic bead, one medium pink frosted, one red frosted and one orange rocaille. Pass the thread back through the first three beads and make a double stitch at the hem.

5 Feed the thread along the hem halfway to the next pin marker and thread on one medium pink frosted bead, one red frosted and one orange rocaille. Pass the thread back through the first two beads and make a double stitch at the hem. Repeat the pattern all around the hem to complete.

6 To make the elaborate trim, begin with a pendant loop consisting of one square orange frosted bead, one small pink frosted, one square orange frosted, one small pink frosted, one square orange frosted, then one large pink frosted and one orange rocaille. Pass the thread back through the large pink frosted and the last square frosted bead and then repeat the sequence for the other side.

7 Make a double stitch at the hem to secure the pendant loop. Make a small loop consisting of one square orange frosted bead, one red frosted, one square orange frosted, one pink frosted and one rocaille. Pass the thread back through the pink frosted bead and then repeat the sequence for the other side.

8 Make a double stitch at the hem to secure the small loop. Continue all around the hem in this way to complete.

BEADED BOAT TAPESTRY

All types of needlework can be further embellished with beadwork; tiny embroidery beads can be incorporated into traditional embroidery or cross-stitch pieces. Here, they are used to add highlights to a tapestry design. The finished design can be framed or made into a cushion.

YOU WILL NEED
10-count tapestry canvas
tapestry frame
drawing pins (thumbtacks) or stapler
ruler
pencil
tapestry yarns in white, red, very pale blue, pale blue, royal blue, jade green, green, yellow, grey, brown and black
tapestry needle
glass embroidery beads in five colours to co-ordinate with the yarn
fine needle and matching sewing thread
scissors
towel or clean cloth
iron
backing card (cardboard)
picture frame

1 Attach the canvas to the tapestry frame using drawing pins (thumbtacks) or staples.

2 Use a ruler to find the centre of the canvas and mark with a pencil. Use this as a starting point to work the design from the chart at the back of the book.

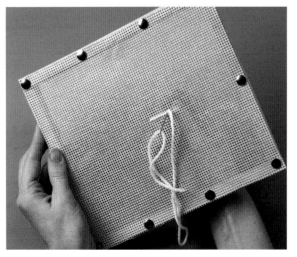

3 Using one strand of tapestry yarn, start to stitch the design using a tent stitch or half cross-stitch, following the chart.

▶

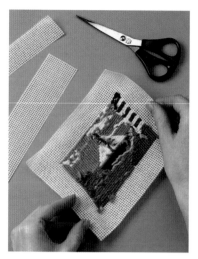

4 When the design is complete, start to add the beads with a fine needle, using them to high-light the waves and other areas of the design. You may find it easier to remove the tapestry from the frame at this stage.

5 Continue to add beads in complementary colours. Finish off the last bead firmly.

6 Measure a 3 cm/1½ in border all around the design, and cut away any excess. Gently stretch the canvas to regain its shape.

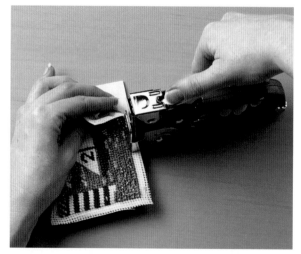

7 Using a towel or folded cloth to cushion your surface, press the tapestry using an iron on a low heat.

8 Cut a piece of backing card (cardboard) 1 cm/½ in larger all round than the tapestry. Staple the tapestry to the backing, trim away any excess canvas, and fit into the frame.

BEADED CUSHION TRIMS

Although these cushion trims appear very delicate, they are stitched along the seams using a strong thread and are unlikely to break. Part of the fun is experimenting with designs: drops and swags always look stunning.

YOU WILL NEED
0.5 m/½ yd each purple and green linen
scissors
tape measure
dressmaker's pins
sewing machine
matching sewing thread
two cushion pads, measuring 35 cm/14 in square and
30 cm/12 in square
graph paper
pencil
fine beading needle
strong non-stretch bead thread
iridescent beads in pink and green
rocaille beads in gold, silver and red
frosted bugle beads in pink, blue and green
green metallic bugle beads
small crystal beads in pink, blue and yellow

1 First make up the cushion covers. Cut a 38 cm/15 in square from the purple linen for the front of the larger cushion, and two pieces for the back measuring 38 x 28 cm/15 x 11 in. For the smaller cushion, cut a 33 cm/13¼ in square and two back pieces measuring 33 x 23 cm/13¼ x 9 in.

2 Stitch a narrow hem across one long edge of each back piece. Place both of these pieces on top of the front piece, right sides together, overlapping the hemmed edges at the centre. Stitch all round the covers with a 1.5 cm/⅝ in seam allowance and turn right-side out. Insert the cushion pads.

3 Decide on the design of the trim, drawing your ideas on a piece of graph paper.

4 The trim for the purple cushion is made up of alternate swags and drops and is stitched along two opposite edges of the cushion. Measure one edge of the cushion and divide it at equidistant points approximately 5 cm/2 in apart. Mark each point vertically with a pin.

5 Begin the trim at the left-hand edge, starting with the beads along the seam to help mark out the position of the swags and drops. Make a small fastening stitch, then thread up an iridescent pink bead followed by a gold rocaille. Take the needle around the last bead, then back through the pink bead, into the cushion seam and back out along the seam beside the pink bead.

6 Thread up a line of pink frosted bugle beads alternating with gold rocaille beads. Take a stitch through the seam about halfway along the line and continue until you reach the first marker pin. Thread up a green iridescent bead followed by a gold rocaille bead in the same manner as for the pink bead. Continue until the line of beads along the seam is complete.

7 The drops and swags can be completed together. Thread up the first drop, inserting the needle just below the pink iridescent bead. Thread up a silver rocaille followed by a blue frosted bugle and repeat. Follow with a silver rocaille, a pink crystal and silver rocaille. Take the needle around the last bead and back up through the rest. Return the needle through the seam line, fasten off and bring it out one bead to the right.

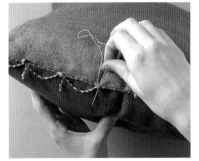

8 Continue with the swag. Thread a silver rocaille followed by a frosted bugle and repeat twice; thread another silver rocaille, a gold rocaille, and a pink crystal. Repeat the beads on the other side of the crystal as a mirror image. Stitch into the seam line and fasten off just under the green iridescent bead. Continue with alternate drops and swags until the trim is complete.

9 The green cushion trim is made up of alternating drops and triangles. Use the same method as before to mark out the seam line with pins, this time at 3 cm/1½ in intervals.

10 Follow the same method as before, but start with the drops and triangles. Thread up the first drop consisting of two red rocailles, a blue frosted bugle, a red rocaille, a green frosted bugle, red rocaille, blue frosted bugle, red rocaille, blue crystal and red rocaille. Take the needle around the last bead and back up through the rest. Fasten off and bring the needle out one bead along.

11 Continue with the triangle. Thread a single red rocaille followed by the same configuration of beads as for the drop. Then, instead of a blue crystal, thread a yellow crystal followed by a red rocaille. This time take the needle around the last bead, back up through the crystal bead only and continue threading the other side of the triangle as a mirror image of the first side. Attach to the seam just to the left of the pin marker, fasten off and continue with alternate drops and triangles until complete.

12 Stitch a line of beads along the seam line, in the gaps left by the triangles. Insert the needle and thread up a gold rocaille, green metallic bugle, three gold rocailles, another bugle and finally a gold rocaille. Stitch at the marker to fasten, then continue until you reach the end of the seam.

BEADED THROW

Brightly painted wooden beads are ideal for fringing a plain cotton throw, as they are light in weight and tend to have large holes. Combine them with the occasional metallic bead to catch the light and give definition to the design.

YOU WILL NEED
florist's wire
wire cutters
ready-made throw with fringe
small, medium and large wooden beads in various colours
brass beads

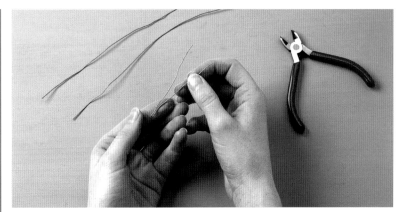

1 Make a threading device by cutting a short length of florist's wire and bending it in two.

2 Decide on the design for your fringe. This throw had 60 lengths of fringe, each knotted at the top. Every other length was beaded with one medium, one small and one large wooden bead and two brass beads, alternating the colours of the large beads. It took 30 small and medium beads, 15 of each of the coloured large beads and 60 brass beads to fringe one end of the throw. Untie the top knot of each length of fringe that is to be beaded. Thread on a brass bead using the wire threader. ▶

3 Twist the fringe to secure stray ends and tie a knot to sit close to the brass bead.

4 Thread on a small bead, then a large bead, a medium bead and finally a brass bead. Tie a knot as before.

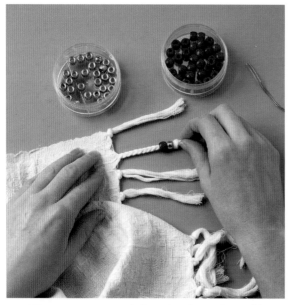

5 There are many variations for decorating a fringe with beads. For example, you could plait (braid) the fringe and add a coloured bead followed by a brass bead.

6 Another idea is to join two lengths of fringe together with one bead. Thread contrasting smaller beads followed by a brass bead to each length of fringe and knot the ends.

FISH MOSAIC SPLASHBACK

Beads clustered together make an original addition to mosaics, and are perfect for creating intricate shapes. Use a mixture of sizes and colours for the fish, and stick to one type of bead for the starfish for a contrasting effect.

YOU WILL NEED
pencil
paper
piece of plywood to fit splashback area
carbon paper
glass mosaic tiles in a variety of colours
wood glue
interior filler
mixing container
spoon
acrylic paints in a variety of colours
selection of beads including metallic bugle beads, frosted and
metallic square beads, large round beads and mixed beads
mosaic clippers
tile grout
cloth

1 Sketch the design to fit the splashback on a large sheet of paper, keeping the shapes simple and bold. Use a sheet of carbon paper to transfer the design to the plywood by drawing firmly over all the lines using a pencil.

2 Apply the mosaic border. Lay out all the tiles first, alternating the colours. Then apply wood glue to the border, a small section at a time, positioning the tiles as you go.

3 Following the manufacturer's instructions, mix up a small amount of interior filler, then add some acrylic paint to colour it to match the beads.

4 Spread green filler thickly over the seaweed fronds, then carefully press in metallic green bugle beads.

5 Fill in the fish fins using green filler and metallic green square beads. Make sure all the beads are on their sides so that the holes don't show. Spread orange filler thickly over the starfish and press in square frosted beads. Use some darker beads for shading.

6 Glue on a large bead for the fish eye using wood glue. Thickly spread white filler onto a 5 cm/2 in square section of the fish body and press in mixed beads. Repeat, working in small sections, until the fish is complete. Glue on large beads for bubbles.

7 For the background and rocks, use mosaic clippers to cut the mosaic tiles into 1 cm/½ in squares.

8 Fill in the background and rocks, varying the shades and sticking the tiles with wood glue. Clip the edges of the tiles where necessary to fit around curved areas of the design. Mix up tile grout following the manufacturer's instructions and spread over the completed design. Spread very lightly and carefully over the beaded areas. Wipe off the grout with a damp cloth and leave to dry.

GLITTERING BEAD SPHERES

Easy and satisfying to make, these spheres look rich and exotic massed together. You could add ribbon loops to make opulent Christmas tree decorations, but the spheres are too pretty to be hidden away for the remainder of the year.

YOU WILL NEED
polystyrene (styrofoam) balls, 5 cm/2 in, 7 cm/2¾ in and
10 cm/4 in diameter
skewer
acrylic paints in blue and green
artist's paintbrushes
long dressmaker's pins
silver-lined glass rocaille beads
round frosted glass beads in assorted sizes in shades of
blue and green
pen or pencil
large faceted sequins in blue and green
small glass rocaille beads in blue and green
round metallic embroidery beads in blue and green

1 Stick the small polystyrene (styrofoam) ball on a skewer to hold it steady while painting. Paint it with a coat of blue acrylic paint and allow to dry. Apply another coat if necessary.

2 With a pin, pick up a small silver-lined rocaille and a larger blue frosted bead and insert in the ball. Pin the beads close together all over the ball.

3 Paint the 7 cm/2¾ in ball green and allow to dry, then use a pen or pencil to mark out a grid pattern as shown.

4 Pin a large green sequin, a large frosted bead and a green rocaille at each crossing point of the grid.

5 Fill in the design with small glass rocailles and tiny embroidery beads. ▶

6 To make the panelled design, paint the large ball blue, allow to dry and, using a pen or pencil, mark out into six equal sections.

7 Pin groups of large sequins, large frosted beads and small rocailles in a row along each line.

8 Fill in each panel with small glass rocailles.

BEADED WALL SCONCE

French-style beaded chandeliers or wall sconces are beautiful but expensive. However, it's easy to create your own: transform a junk shop or fleamarket find with the help of gold paint, wire and swags of cheap but effective plastic crystal beads.

YOU WILL NEED
wall sconce
metallic gold paint
medium paintbrush
stiff card (cardboard)
pair of compasses (compass)
scissors
thick needle
wire cutters
fine brass wire
medium-sized transparent plastic crystal bead drops
round-nosed jewellery pliers
transparent plastic crystal beads
large and small coloured beads

1 Paint the sconce gold to give a gilded effect. Leave to dry. You may need more than one coat to achieve good coverage.

2 Cut two discs of stiff card (cardboard). These will be inserted in the joints where the sconce arms unscrew to allow for wiring, so should be a little wider than the arms at this point. Paint the discs gold and leave to dry. Cut out the centres to fit around the wires. Make a cut from the edge to the centre of each so that it can be opened, then use a thick needle to punch three equidistant holes between the inner and outer edges.

3 Make up three bead drops for each disc. The links are made with individual lengths of wire to give flexibility. Using the wire cutters, cut a piece of wire about 3 cm/1½ in long. Thread on the base crystal drop bead and use the pliers to twist the wire once. Leave the ends open.

▶

4 Take a second length of wire of about the same length and make a small closed loop at one end using the pliers. Slip this loop over one of the open ends of the previous wire and twist the open ends together to secure the link. Trim the excess wire.

5 Thread on a medium-sized transparent bead. Cut the wire to 8 mm/⅜ in and make another closed loop. Cut another length of wire, thread it through and make another closed loop. Thread on a small coloured bead. Repeat the looping process to add one more medium transparent bead. Add the final length of wire.

6 Repeat steps 3–5 for the remaining drops. Attach the drops to the gold-painted discs, looping the wires through the punched holes.

7 Decide where the swags will be positioned on the sconce and measure the swagged length between the two points. Make up the swags using the same looped wire method as before, alternating a medium transparent bead with a small coloured bead. At the centre of the swag, place a large coloured bead as a focal point.

8 Attach the swags by wrapping the ends of the wire around the arms of the sconce at least twice and twisting. Fit the gold discs in the joints of the sconce arms.

MONOGRAMMED BAG

This simple little drawstring bag is made more personal with a pair of initials worked in tiny embroidery beads couched in place. A small bag of this size could be used for holding shoes or accessories, while a larger bag for laundry could be made to match.

YOU WILL NEED
60 x 25 cm/24 x 10 in rectangle of cotton, silk or linen, for the bag
60 x 25 cm/24 x 10 in rectangle of cotton lawn or lightweight silk, for lining
tape measure
dressmaker's scissors
pencil and tracing paper or vanishing fabric marker
beading needle
matching sewing thread
glass embroidery beads in a variety of colours
small glass bugle beads
dressmaker's pins
sewing machine
100 cm/40 in silk or leather cord
safety pin
2 large beads with large centre holes

1 Cut two rectangles each from the main fabric and lining fabric, measuring 30 x 25 cm/12 x 10 in. Draw your chosen initials freehand onto a piece of tracing paper. Rub over the wrong side of the tracing paper, and place the paper right side up over the right side of one of the main pieces of fabric. Trace over the lines to transfer the design to the main fabric.

2 If the lines are too faint, re-trace directly on the fabric with a pencil or vanishing fabric marker. Alternatively, draw the design directly onto the fabric with the fabric marker.

3 Thread the beading needle and fasten the thread firmly to the main fabric. Bring the needle out at the top of the first initial. Thread the needle with enough glass embroidery beads to complete a single line on the monogram.

55

4 Couch the first line in place. Continue until you have completed the whole monogram, and fasten off (secure) the thread.

5 Decorate the rest of the bag with individual embroidery beads and small bugles in a variety of colours.

6 To make up the bag, pin the two main pieces right sides together, and machine-stitch along three sides, leaving the top open. Repeat with the lining fabric. Turn the main fabric right-side out, and press.

7 Slip the lining inside the bag. Fold all raw edges inside, pin, and slip-stitch the folded edge of the lining to the folded edge of the bag. Sew two lines of stitching through both thicknesses of fabric, 3 cm/ 1¼ in and 1 cm/½ in from the top edge of the bag, to form the channel for the drawstrings.

8 At each side, snip through the stitches of the side seams between the two rows, to make a gap to insert the cords. Cut the cord in half. Use a safety pin to help you thread one half right through from one side, and the other from the opposite side. Thread a decorative bead onto the two cords at each side, and knot to secure.

STRAWBERRY PINCUSHION

Elaborately beaded pincushions were very popular among Victorian ladies, and are very simple yet effective to make. This method can be adapted to suit other designs and decorations, and can be made as a gift with the recipient's initials.

YOU WILL NEED
small piece of red velvet
dressmaker's pins
dressmaker's scissors
tape measure
vanishing fabric marker
needle and matching sewing thread
sawdust or bran, for stuffing
small glass rocaille beads in
green and red
white pearlized beads
green sequins
scrap of green ribbon

1 Trace the template from the back of the book, cut out, and trace round onto the wrong side of the velvet using the vanishing fabric marker.

2 Cut out the two strawberry shapes. Cut a strip of velvet for the gusset, 21 x 2.5 cm/ 8½ x 1 in.

3 Join the two ends of the gusset strip, right sides together, stitching the seam in back stitch and leaving a seam allowance of a scant 3-4 mm/⅛ in.

4 With right sides together, stitch the two strawberry shapes to the gusset, leaving a small gap on one side.

5 Turn right-side out and stuff firmly with sawdust or bran.

6 Tuck in the raw edges of the opening, and slip-stitch neatly to close.

7 Decorate the strawberry with beads and sequins. Start at the top, by threading a green bead and sequin onto a pin, then fixing into the pincushion. Work the beads and sequins in a leaf shape.

8 Continue decorating the pincushion with red rocaille beads interspersed with the white pearlized beads to represent seeds. Finally, pin or stitch a loop of green ribbon to the top of the pincushion.

BEAD PENDANT LIGHT

This whimsical lampshade gives you the perfect opportunity to sort through your collection of beads and use all your prettiest shapes in rainbow colours. Use a large crystal drop at the bottom of each strand to give weight to the fringe.

YOU WILL NEED
enamel spray-paint
scrap paper
flush pendant lamp ring
fine jewellery wire (this design used about 20 m/22 yd)
scissors
large crystal drop beads
medium round and shaped beads
bugle beads

1 Spray-paint the lamp ring on a piece of scrap paper in a well-ventilated area and leave it to dry.

2 Cut a piece of jewellery wire a little more than twice the length you want the finished fringe and thread on a large crystal drop bead.

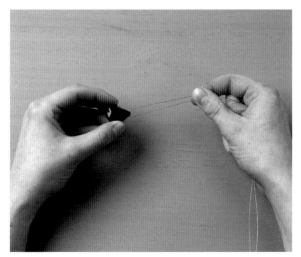

3 Take the bead to the centre of the length of wire and hold the two ends together.

4 Thread on an assortment of beads in different sizes and colours, spacing them with bugle beads. ▶

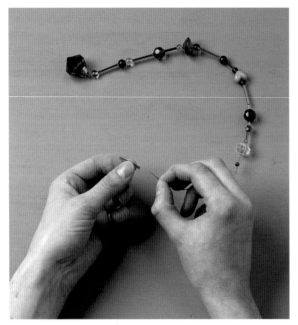

5 Complete the strand with a long bugle bead, making sure you have left enough wire to tie onto the lamp ring.

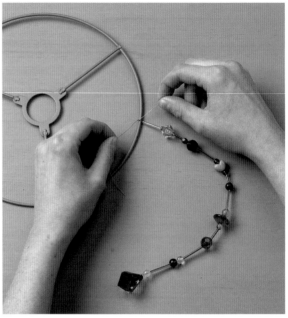

6 Attach the strand of beads onto the ring, by tying the two ends of the wire together.

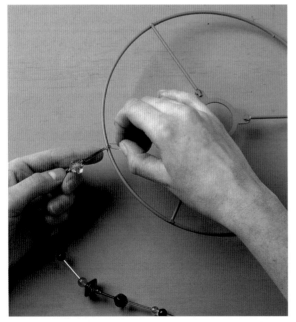

7 Thread the two wire ends back through the beads to conceal them.

8 Continue making beaded strands to tie evenly all around the metal ring.

LACY BOTTLE COLLARS

You can turn plain glass bottles into jewelled treasures with these exquisite beaded collars. Fill them with anything from bath salts to home-made liqueurs to make wonderful gifts. There are two designs to choose from.

YOU WILL NEED
strong, non-stretch bead thread
beading needle
small glass rocaille beads in lime, lilac
and dark green
glass bottles
glass bugle beads in green and lilac
small, medium and large faceted glass
crystals in green and lilac
small pearlized embroidery beads in
green and lilac
large dark green glass rocaille beads
lilac glass drops

1 Take a long piece of beading thread and begin with one row of alternate small lime and lilac rocailles long enough to fit around the bottle neck. Tie it securely around the neck.

2 Passing the thread through each bead of the first row again, thread on a green bugle and a lime rocaille. Return the thread through the bugle, then pass through the next bead in the ring and repeat with a lilac bugle.

3 Pass the thread through the lime rocailles and pull it tightly to form a collar to cover the neck of the bottle.

4 Passing the thread through every other green rocaille at the base of the collar, thread on a green bugle, a lilac rocaille, a green bugle, a medium lilac crystal and a green embroidery bead. Pass the thread through the crystal again and repeat the sequence on the other side to return to the collar. Make pendant loops all round the bottle, alternating the green and lilac colour sequences as shown. Finish the end of the thread securely. Neaten any loose threads by passing them back through the last few beads.

5 To make the more complex collar, begin with a row of alternate small dark green and lilac rocailles tied securely around the bottle neck. Then, passing the thread through the green rocailles only, thread on a green bugle and a lilac rocaille. Pass the thread again through the bugle and then the next green rocaille and continue around the neck.

6 Pass the thread through each lilac rocaille, adding a small dark green rocaille between each. Pull the thread up tightly to form the neck collar and tie securely.

7 Passing the thread through alternate lilac rocailles, add pendant loops consisting of three lime rocailles, a small dark green rocaille, then three more lime rocailles.

8 Passing the thread between each small dark green rocaille of the previous round, make another round of loops, consisting of one lilac bugle, a green embroidery bead, a small green crystal, a green embroidery bead and a lilac bugle. ▶

9 Passing the thread through the small green crystals of the previous loops, make loops consisting of three small dark green rocailles, one lilac embroidery bead, one medium lilac crystal, one lilac embroidery bead and three small dark green rocailles.

10 Passing the thread between the lilac crystals of the previous round, make links consisting of one lilac embroidery bead, one green embroidery bead, one green bugle, one green embroidery bead and one lilac embroidery bead.

11 Passing the thread between the lilac crystals again, make loops consisting of one lilac embroidery bead, three small dark green rocailles, one small lilac crystal, three green rocailles and one lilac embroidery bead.

12 Passing the thread between the small lilac crystals of the previous loops, make a final round of pendant loops consisting of one small dark green rocaille, one green or lilac bugle, one small dark green rocaille, one large dark green rocaille, one large green or lilac crystal, one small dark green rocaille and one lilac drop. Then pass back through the small dark green rocaille, crystal and large rocaille and repeat the sequence for the other side. Tie the threads off securely, threading any ends back through the last few beads neatly.

CHUNKY BEAD TIE-BACKS

Use large glass beads in strong colours to make tie-backs that will become the focal points of your window decoration. Before you begin, gather up the curtain in the loop of a tape measure to judge the perfect length for the tie-backs.

YOU WILL NEED
For each tie-back:
2 keyrings
2 decorative dividers with attachments for three strings
glue gun and glue sticks
4 flat-backed blue glass nuggets
scissors
pencil
paper for template
strong non-stretch bead thread
clear nail polish
cylindrical orange hand-made glass and ceramic beads
round blue glass beads
large blue glass beads

1 Attach a keyring to each divider to loop over the wall hooks.

2 Using a glue gun and glue sticks, attach a glass nugget to each divider.

3 Draw and cut out a paper template of the tie-back to fit your curtain and use as a rough guide when threading up the beads. Pass a length of bead thread through the top loop of one divider and tie in ▶ a double knot.

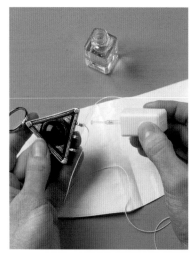

4 Set the knot with a little clear nail polish.

5 Thread on beads using the picture as a guide to the sequence. Pass both the main length of thread and the spare end through the first few beads.

6 Complete the first row to fit the template and knot to the other divider in the same way, setting the knot with nail varnish as before.

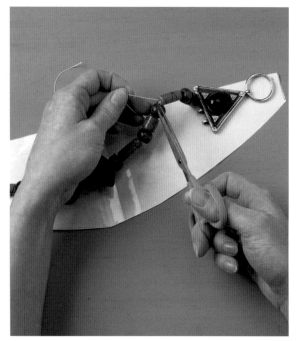

7 Pass the spare end of thread back through the last few beads and snip off.

8 Thread up the second and third rows following the same sequence, adding extra beads to make each row a little longer than the previous one. Repeat for the other tie-back.

BEAD-ENCRUSTED APPLIQUÉ FLOWER

Beads add texture and detail to this child-like, stylized flower decoration for a loose chair cover. In a design of strong shapes and colour contrasts, created in sturdy fabrics, their delicacy creates a delightful surprise.

YOU WILL NEED
iron
fusible bonding web
scraps of cotton fabrics in three colours
card (cardboard) for template
pencil
scissors
sewing machine
matching sewing threads
beading needle
small glass rocaille beads
bugle beads
assorted round glass beads
canvas chair cover
dressmaker's pins
needle and tacking (basting) thread

1 Iron fusible bonding web to the wrong side of the fabrics you have chosen for the flower appliqué.

2 Copy the templates at the back of the book for the petal and flower centre. Draw around the petal template on the backing paper and cut out 12 shapes. Cut out the circular centre for the flower from a contrasting fabric.

3 Arrange the petals on a square of the background fabric, peel off the backing paper and iron them in place. Iron on the flower centre.

▶

71

4 Stitch around the shapes using a decorative stitch such as zig-zag stitch or satin stitch.

5 Decorate the flower centre and petals with an assortment of evenly spaced glass rocaille and bugle beads.

6 Fold in the raw edges of the background square and press in place.

7 Following the folded seam line, sew on an assortment of small and medium-sized round glass beads in various assorted colours, stitching them about 1 cm/½ in apart.

8 Position the appliqué panel on the back of the chair cover. Pin and tack (baste) it in place, then machine-stitch it close to the edge.

WOVEN BEAD TRIM

Investing in a simple bead loom will enable you to weave fabulous patterns, reminiscent of the traditional decorative art of Native Americans. You can make the trim as long as you need, winding the panel around the spool as it grows.

YOU WILL NEED
bead loom
strong, non-stretch bead thread
tape measure
scissors
fine beading needle
small opaque rocaille beads in four colours
adhesive tape (optional)

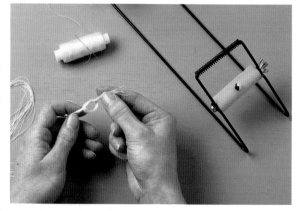

1 To thread the loom, first cut 19 strands of bead thread to the length of the finished panel plus 40 cm/16 in. (There is always one more strand than the number of beads in a row.) Tie all the ends in a knot.

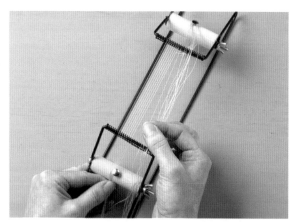

2 Divide the threads into two equal bundles and place the knot over the nail head on the wooden spool at the top of the loom, then slip each thread into one of the grooves in the separator spring.

3 Wind the threads carefully onto the top spool, and tie the ends around the nail head on the wooden spool at the other end.

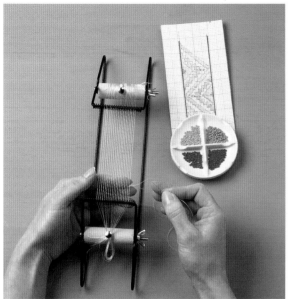

4 Thread the beading needle and tie the end of the thread in a double knot to the right-hand warp (lengthways) thread on the loom.

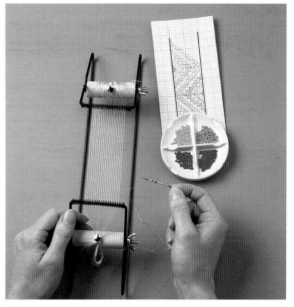

5 Following the chart at the back of the book, pick up coloured beads on the needle to correspond with the first row of the pattern.

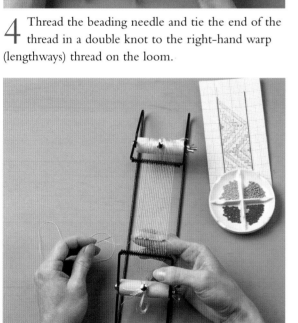

6 Place the beads under the warp threads and, using your finger, press a bead between each of the warp threads.

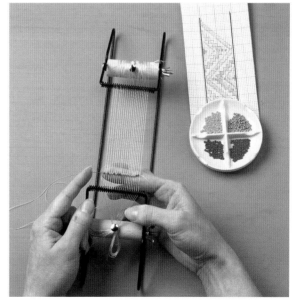

7 Pass the needle back through the beads, being sure to pass over the warp threads. Continue following the chart row by row until you have the desired length of trim.

▶

8 To finish, weave the beading thread under and over the warp threads for a short distance to secure the beads. Tape or stitch this woven part behind the trim before attaching it.

Note

To add on a new weft thread, tie to the right-hand warp thread as before. Weave any loose threads into the rows of beads to conceal them.

JEWELLED LAMPSHADES

Transparent glass beads naturally belong with light and make perfect lampshade decorations. Turn plain, inexpensive shades into light-hearted works of art with these bright ideas that are all quick and simple to do.

YOU WILL NEED
beading needle
matching sewing threads
grosgrain ribbon
small glass rocaille beads in mauve,
red and blue
long and short bugle beads in blue
3 lampshades
strong glue
masking tape
ricrac braid
iron
fusible bonding web
scraps of plain silk in three colours
scrap paper
scissors
pencil
PVA (white) glue
medium paintbrush
marker pen or pencil
craft knife
handmade paper

1 For the fringed lampshade, thread the needle, tying a strong knot in the end, and thread it through one end of the ribbon. Thread up one mauve rocaille and one red rocaille, a short blue bugle bead, one mauve rocaille, a long blue bugle bead and five rocailles in the following sequence: blue, mauve, red, mauve, red. When you have threaded the final bead, take the needle back through the other beads until you reach the top. Make a fastening-off (securing) stitch in the ribbon.

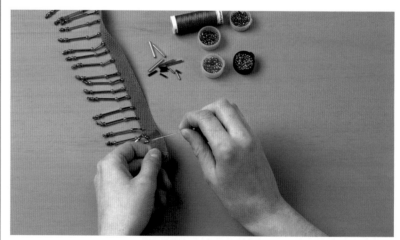

2 Decide on the spacing between the drops of the fringe and sew a few running stitches along the ribbon, then repeat the sequence until you have the required length of beaded fringing.

3 Glue the ricrac braid around the outside edge of the lampshade and leave to dry.

4 Glue the beaded fringing to the inside edge of the lampshade, overlapping the ends by 1 cm/½ in and turning in the raw edge of the ribbon. Hold in place with masking tape while the glue dries.

5 For the starry lampshade, iron fusible bonding web onto the wrong side of the silk. Peel off the backing paper and iron the fabric onto scrap paper.

6 Draw a star freehand to make a template. Draw around it on the paper backing and cut out several stars from each colour silk.

7 Sew rocaille beads evenly over the surface of each star, using matching thread.

▶

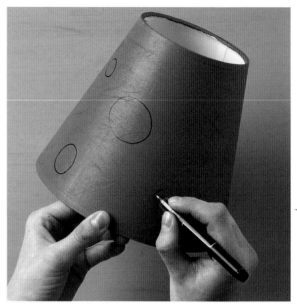

8 Arrange the stars around the lampshade, then use PVA (white) glue to stick them in place.

9 Mark out circular holes for the third shade using a marker pen or pencil. Cut out the holes using a craft knife.

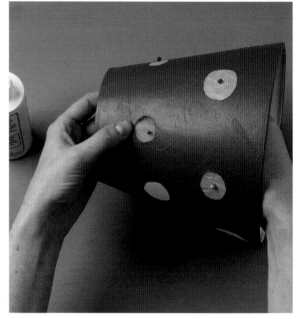

10 Cut or tear the handmade paper into small pieces and sew a small rocaille bead in the centre of each piece.

11 Paint a small amount of PVA glue around each hole on the inside of the shade and stick the pieces of paper in place.

BEADS

Beads come in a large variety of sizes, shapes, colours and finishes. Here is a simple breakdown of the names and types of beads most commonly available today.

BUGLE BEADS These glass tubes are most commonly available in sizes 2 mm (⅛ in) to 35 mm (1½ in). The surface can be smooth or faceted, in a range of finishes.

CERAMIC AND PORCELAIN BEADS These often have intricate hand-painted patterns and designs. They usually have a large hole, making them useful for thick cord.

CUT GLASS AND CRYSTAL BEADS These come in a variety of shapes and cuts of facet. Some have mirror-finished facets.

CUT PLASTIC BEADS These are much cheaper than glass versions although not quite as bright.

METAL BEADS Brass, copper, steel and aluminium beads, as well as silver and gold-plated ones are available in a vast range of styles.

ROCAILLES OR SMALL GLASS BEADS These are the most commonly available beads. The overall term "rocailles" is further divided into round and faceted rocailles. The finishes may be pearlized, lustre, metallic, iridescent or silver-lined.

SEQUINS These shiny discs of thin flat or faceted metal or plastic can be used with a small glass bead fixed over the sequin's central hole.

SPECIAL AND FOUND BEADS Apart from the main classifications of beads listed, there are many more types and designs to choose from, such as recycled glass, Venetian glass, foiled, iridescent, square, flower-shaped and Indian. There are also beads made from natural objects such as seeds, nuts and shells. You can make beads by drilling a small hole in your own found objects.

WOODEN BEADS Available in a natural finish or stained, they can be polished, carved and painted. They tend to be quite economical, particularly in the larger sizes.

Opposite: 1) Large and small rocailles in opaque, pearlized, metallic and lined finishes. 2) Large and small bugle beads in opaque and metallic finishes. 3) Plastic cut beads in a variety of colours. 4) Faceted sequins. 5) Matt glass flower beads. 6) Painted and stained wooden beads in all shapes and sizes. 7) Metal beads in a variety of finishes and designs. 8) Recycled glass beads. 9) Mix of decorative glass beads. 10) Iridescent finished beads. 11) Large plastic pearlized beads, lampwork glass beads. 12) Cut glass beads. 13) Square glass beads. 14) Foiled glass beads.

4

5

2

1

3

6

2

14

8

9

7

1

MATERIALS

*The materials needed for beadwork are available from good
department stores, art and craft shops as well as specialized
bead shops and mail order companies.*

COVERED BUTTONS Buttons that can be covered in fabric and then beaded are used for trimming customized soft furnishings.

DRINKING STRAWS These make inexpensive and decorative space fillers for large bead curtains.

FABRIC Many beadwork projects are attached or applied to fabric. Any fabric can be used, from thick cottons to fine silks and linens, depending on its ultimate purpose.

POLYMER CLAY This clay is available in many colours and designs and is ideal for making up your own large or small beads.

POLYSTYRENE (STYROFOAM) BALLS These balls are used as a base for making up beaded and sequinned balls; pins are pressed into the ball to attach the beads.

RIBBON, BRAID AND FABRIC TAPE Ribbons and braids can be used for embellishing soft beaded objects or used as a decorative tape to apply fringe to. Ordinary fabric tape can be used to attach fringing where it will not show.

SILK CORDS, THREADS AND LEATHER THONGS There is a variety of cords and threads available for threading up larger beads for decorative purposes. These come in an extensive range of widths and colours. Embroidery thread (floss) can be used for making beaded tassels.

TAPESTRY CANVAS Use canvas of the size required as a base for straightforward tapestry which you can then embellish with beads.

THREADS Ordinary cotton thread is useful for threading and stitching beads that do not require reinforced strength. Polyester threads are used for beadwork that requires more strength, such as fringing. Nylon thread and synthetic fishing line are useful when you require a transparent thread.

WIRE Fine wires specifically for beading come in copper, brass and silver finishes. Electrical fuse wire can also be used.

*Opposite: 1) Various fabrics and
tapestry canvas. 2) Ribbon and braid.
3) Fabric tape. 4) Polymer clay.
5) Drinking straws. 6) Cotton
thread. 7) Wire. 8) Silk thread.
9) Uncovered buttons. 10) Polystyrene
(styrofoam) balls. 11) Silk cord.
12) Leather thongs. 13) Embroidery
thread. 14) Transparent nylon wire.
15) Polyester thread.*

5

11

2

3

25mm x 1.5m

4

7

8

9

10

13

Ancl

433

14

15

EQUIPMENT

There are few pieces of equipment needed for beadwork, and as the majority of beading involves some sort of threading, the most important item is the needle. The other items particular to beadwork comprise a bead loom, for certain types of woven beading, and tools for working with wire.

BEAD LOOM Available from specialist bead shops, this loom enables you to weave strips of solid beadwork. The design is plotted onto a piece of graph paper and translated onto the loom.

DRESSMAKER'S PINS Pins can be used for marking up designs such as the edge of a cushion trimming.

EMBROIDERY HOOP Use a hoop for stretching fabric or tapestry canvas to make any fine bead embroidery easier to handle.

GRAPH PAPER This is ideal for drawing out and plotting designs for fringing, trimming and bead loom work.

NEEDLES The size and type of needle that you use depends on the size of hole in the bead, the thread you wish to use, and the type of project you are undertaking. The best thing to do is experiment. Fine standard needles or millinery needles are often ideal. Beading needles are available in many sizes but because they are long and fine they tend to break and should be used for more delicate work. However, the length of the needle is useful for threading up lots of beads at a time. For threading up thicker threads or cord and larger beads, florist's wire bent double and twisted will work very well. There are also "threaders" available from specialist shops for this purpose.

PLIERS Used for cutting or forming loops in wire. Round-nosed pliers are perfect for forming loops when beads are threaded onto wire and then linked together.

SCISSORS A good pair of sharp scissors is needed for most projects involving beads, for cutting thread or fine wire.

STAPLE GUN Stapling is a quick and easy way of securing completed items such as a ribbon along the top of a fine bead curtain.

TAPE MEASURE AND RULER Some designs, where beads should be placed at measured intervals require accurate measuring and marking up.

Opposite: 1) Bead loom. 2) Regular and pearl-headed pins. 3) Tape measure. 4) "Threaders". 5) Needles. 6) Graph paper. 7) Embroidery hoop. 8) Florist's wire. 9) Staple gun. 10) Scissors. 11) Pliers. 12) Ruler.

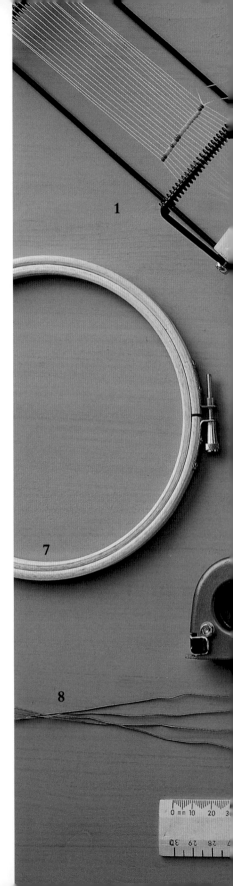

BASIC TECHNIQUES

Many of the techniques used in beadwork are quite straightforward. Work your way slowly
through the instructions below to familiarize yourself with the methods.

SECURING BEADS

To fasten off (secure) a string or a
single bead, pass the needle under
the main thread to form a loop
beneath this thread. Take the
needle over the top of the main
thread and down into the loop.
Pull tightly.

NEEDLEWOVEN BEADING FOR DECORATIVE TRIMS

This technique involves interlacing
beads using a needle and a single
length of thread to achieve a solid
strip of beads. The strip can be
shaped by increasing or decreasing
the number of beads in a row or
given texture using varying sizes of
beads. It is also known as diagonal
bead weaving and is ideal for
diagonal patterns. Designs should
be charted on a piece of graph
paper before starting.

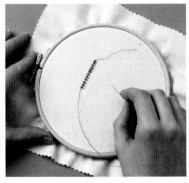

1 Lay down the first row of
beads to the width of your
design by threading them onto a
beading needle and a long length
of thread. The beads can be strung
out on a cork board, secured by
two pins, or stitched to a piece of
fabric at either end as shown.

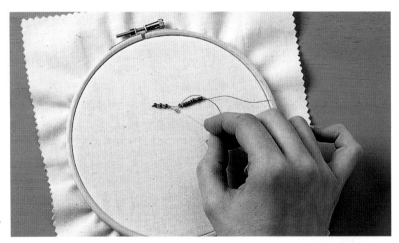

2 Pass the needle and thread back through the first bead. Thread on a
new bead to sit between the first and second beads of the original
row. Pass the needle through the second bead of the original row, thread
on a new bead to sit between the second and third beads of this row and
so on. The last new bead should sit after the last bead of the original row.

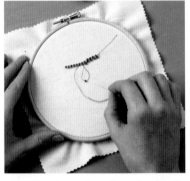

3 Continue threading the third
row to sit between the pairs
of beads in the second row. Once
you have got the hang of beading
straight strips, try increasing and
decreasing to form shapes such as
triangles and curves.

FRINGING

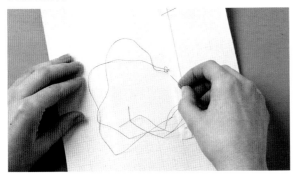

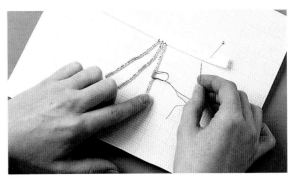

1 If your design is complicated, chart it on graph paper first. A long fringe needs to be very secure so it is advisable to attach the lengths individually. For ease, work the fringe on fabric tape pinned to a cork board, which can be attached to the object afterwards. The bead hole needs to be large enough to hold four thicknesses of bead thread. Decide on the length of fringe and for each length cut a piece of thread to four times that measurement. Double the thread and thread the two ends onto a needle. Stitch the ends through the edge of the tape and through the loop where the thread is doubled. Pull tight.

2 Thread on the beads for the fringe strand, then return the needle over the final bead and back up through half the beads. Make a fastening-off stitch about halfway up the length of the beads, then carry on passing the needle up through the beads. Make another fastening-off stitch about three beads from the top. Pull the thread gently to make sure the beads are hanging smoothly and snip off the ends of the thread.

3 For a short fringe, the beads can be attached with a continuous thread. Work out the amount of thread needed by doubling each length and adding another half extra for fastening on and off (securing). This method can be worked directly onto the fabric but it may be easier to pin it to a cork board. Work from left to right of the design. Attach the thread to the fabric and thread on the first length of beads.

4 Return the thread around the last bead and pass the needle back up through the strand. Fasten off through the fabric and start the next strand one bead width to the right of the first. Continue, following the design until the fringe is completed.

FINISHING DROPS OR FRINGING

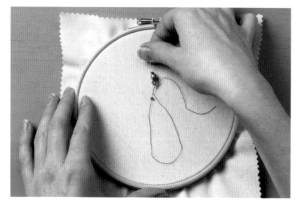 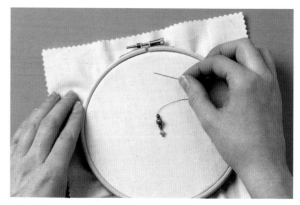

1 This is the easiest and neatest way to finish a length of fringe or a drop. Simply use a small single bead as an anchor. Thread on the beads required for the drop. Thread on the final bead. Then pass the needle around this bead and back up through the previously threaded beads.

2 Drops can be further embellished by forming an anchor from more than one bead. This time thread on the beads required for the drop, then thread on three more beads and pass the needle back up through the final bead of the drop. The three small beads form what is called a "picot" finish.

BEADED BUTTONS

1 For a random design on a fabric-covered button, make a concealed fastening-on (securing) stitch and bring the needle out through the fabric on the button. Thread on a rocaille bead and then make a small stitch and pass the needle back under the fabric. Bring it out a couple of bead-widths away and repeat until the button is covered.

2 For a flower design, make a concealed fastening-on stitch and stitch the main bead in the centre of the button. Divide the circumference of the button into equal parts and make small marks on the outside of the button with a pencil. Stitch a line of beads from the middle bead to each marked point, securing in the centre of the line as you go for extra strength. Secure the thread at the end of each line.

COUCHED BEADING

This technique is ideal for stitching beads to fabric as it results in a smoother effect and a neater continuous line than stitching down each bead individually. It is ideal for fine beadwork and can be used to work a solid motif which can be transferred and appliquéd onto another fabric.

1 First draw your design in pencil as a guide for laying down the beads.

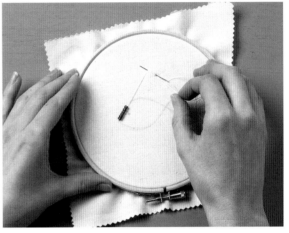

2 Lay down the beads pre-strung on a length of thread and secure in a straight line following the design, with the thread pulled taut around the needle.

3 With a separate length of thread in another needle, stitch over the original thread, working tiny stitches between each bead. After each stitch slide the bead up close so that it sits neatly next to its neighbour and continue stitching. Follow the line of the design, moving and securing the original thread as you go.

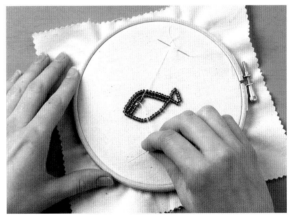

4 For a solid motif, lay the next line as close as possible to the first line and introduce other coloured beads or different shaped beads according to your design.

MAKING YOUR OWN BEADS

It is possible to make your own beads and one of the easiest ways to do this is with polymer clay. This comes in a large range of colours, including multi-coloured designs enabling you to make patterns with ease. Both are particularly useful for making large beads – which can be expensive – and beads with large threading holes, which are quite hard to come by.

1 Plain coloured beads can be made up by simply rolling clay. For marbled beads, take small amounts of different coloured clay and roll together into a ball.

2 Pierce a hole through the centre of the bead using a large needle.

3 To make up patterned beads from multi-coloured clay, first roll the bead shapes in layers of plain clay, one colour on top of another.

4 Using a craft knife, cut very thin slices from the roll of multi-coloured clay.

5 Press the slices on to the surface of the plain beads, completely or partially covering the surface as you wish.

6 Roll the beads again in your hands to smooth out the surface. Pierce holes through the centres with a large needle. Place all the finished beads in an oven to harden according to the manufacturer's instructions.

TEMPLATES

Enlarge the templates on a photocopier if necessary, or trace the design and draw a grid of evenly

spaced squares over your tracing. Draw a larger grid onto another piece of paper and copy the

outline square by square. Draw over the lines to make sure they are continuous.

For the charts, each square represents one bead or a tapestry stitch.

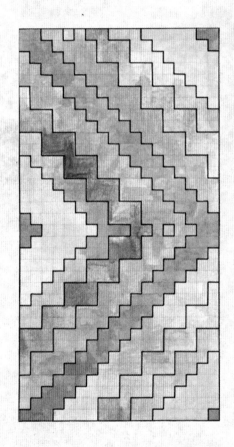

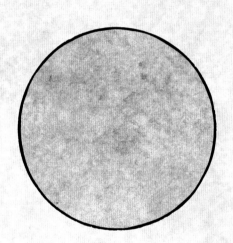

Bead-encrusted Appliqué Flower pp 71-73

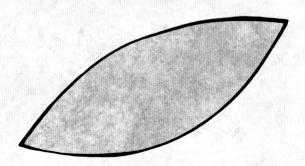

Woven Bead Trim pp74-77

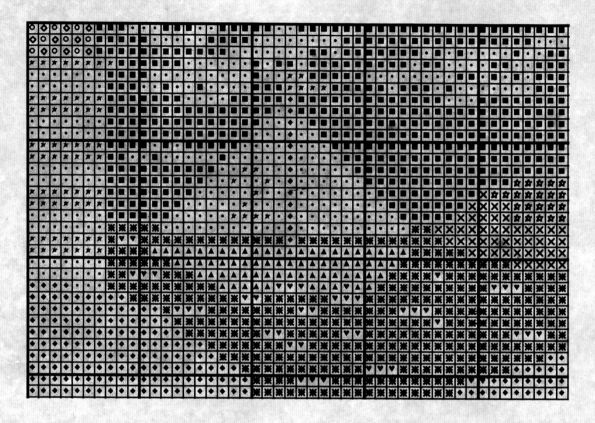

Beaded Boat Tapestry pp35-37

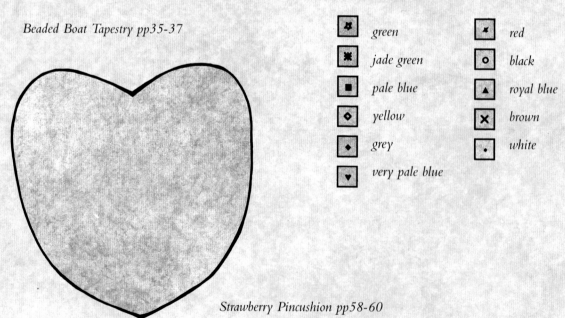

green		red	
jade green		black	
pale blue		royal blue	
yellow		brown	
grey		white	
very pale blue			

Strawberry Pincushion pp58-60

SUPPLIERS

UNITED KINGDOM
The Bead Shop
43 Neal Street,
London WC2H 9PJ
Tel: 0181 553 3240 for catalogue
and mail order enquiries

Beads
259 Portobello Road,
London W11 1LR
Tel: 0171 792 3436

Creative Beadcraft
20 Beak Street,
London W1R 3HA
Tel: 0171 629 9964 or 01494
715606 for catalogue and mail
order enquiries

**The Northern Beading
Company**
The Corn Exchange, Call Lane,
Leeds West Yorkshire LS1 7BR
Tel: 0113 244 3033 for catalogue
and mail order enquiries

UNITED STATES
Discount Bead House
P.O. Box 186, The Plains,
OH 45780
Tel: (800) 793-7592

**S & S Education: Suppliers &
Activities for Creative
Teaching**
P.O. Box 513, Colchester,
CT 06415-0513
Tel: (800) 243-9232

Ornamental Resources, Inc.
P.O. Box 3010, Idaho Springs,
CO 80452
Tel: (303) 567-4988

Shipwreck Beads
5021 Mud Bay Road, Olympia,
WA 98502
Tel: (800) 950-4232

CANADA
Dressew
337 W Hastings Street
Vancouver, BC
Tel: 682 6196

AUSTRALIA
Lincraft
Stores in every capital city except
Darwin. Tel: (03) 9875 7575 for
store addresses

ACKNOWLEDGEMENTS

The author and publishers would like to thank the following for their contribution to this title:

The contributors: Petra Boase (Bead-encrusted Frames, Beaded Appliqué Flower, Bead Pendant Light, Jewelled Lampshades);
Alison Jenkins (Giant Bead Cord-pulls, Napkin Ring and Night-light, Silken Key Tassels, Bead-trimmed Voile Jug Covers,
Glittering Bead Spheres, Lacy Bottle Collars, Chunky Bead Tie-backs, Woven Bead Trim) and Susie Johns (Beaded Boat Tapestry,
Monogrammed Bag, Strawberry Pincushion).

The Bead Shop, 43 Neal Street, London WC2H 9PJ, for providing beads for photography.

Thank you also to the following for lending props for photography: Damask, 3–4 Broxholme House, New King's Road,
corner of Harwood Road, London SW6, and Units 7 & 10, Sulivan Enterprise Centre, Sulivan Road, London SW6;
Elephant, 169–171 Queensway, London W2; Nice Irma's, 46 Goodge Street, London W1; Paperchase, 213 Tottenham Court Road,
London W1; The Pier, 200 Tottenham Court Road, London W1; The Source, 26–40 Kensington High Street, London W8.

INDEX